WHAT IS WEATHER?

Watching the Weather

Miranda Ashwell and Andy Owen

Heinemann Library
Chicago, Illinois

Printed and bound in Hong Kong
Designed by David Oakley
Illustrations by Jeff Edwards

06 05 04
10 9 8 7

Library of Congress Cataloging-in-Publication Data
Owen, Andy, 1961-
    Watching the weather / Andy Owen and Miranda Ashwell.
        p. cm. – (What is weather?)
    Summary: Discusses the need for weather prediction, how certain types of weather are measured, and how
weather patterns are observed.
    ISBN: 1-57572-792-7 (HC), 1-4034-0065-2 (Pbk.)
    Weather–Juvenile literature. 2. Weather forecasting–Juvenile
literature. 3. Meteorology–Juvenile literature. [1. Weather.
2. Weather forecasting. 3. Meteorology.] I. Ashwell, Miranda,
. II. Title. III. Series: Owen, Andy, 1961- What is weather?

QC981.3.O84 1999
551.'3–dc21
                                                                98-42871
                                                                CIP
                                                                AC

Acknowledgments
The author and publishers are grateful to the following for permission to reproduce copyright material:
Austin J. Brown, p. 12; Bruce Coleman Limited, pp. 15, 23; F. Labhardt, p. 5 top; Pacific Stock, p. 8;
Robert Harding Picture Library, pp. 4 top, 11, 26; M. Black, p. 7; J. Greenberg/MR, p. 13; T. Jones, p. 9;
G. White, p. 17; Oxford Scientific Films/NASA, p. 20; Andy Owen, p. 14; Panos Pictures/A. Nelson, p. 25;
Pictor International, p. 16; Rex Features/London, pp. 28, 29; Science Photo Library/M. Burnett, p. 1;
Earth Satellite Corporation, p. 21; NASA, p. 24; NRSC Ltd., p. 10; D. Parker, p. 19; Eurelios/P. Plailly, p. 27;
Stock Market, p. 5 bottom; B. Harris, p. 22; R. Morsch, p. 4 bottom.

Cover photograph: P. Menzel/Science Photo Library.

Every effort has been made to contact copyright holders of any material reproduced in this
book. Any omissions will be rectified in subsequent printings if notice is given to the publisher.

Some words are shown in bold, **like this.** You can find out what
they mean by looking in the glossary.

Contents

What Is Weather?

Rain, sunshine, snow, and wind are all types of weather. We also use the words *hot* and *cold* when we talk about weather.

We all feel the weather. On very wet days, we must wear **waterproof** clothes. On warm, sunny days, we like to be outside.

What Will the Weather Be Like?

We need to know what the weather will be like. It must be dry to play some sports. Rain has stopped this game of tennis.

The sea can be dangerous in windy weather. Before people go out to fish, they need to know that the weather will be safe.

Weather Stories

For hundreds of years, people have wanted to know about the weather. One old story says a red sky at night means that the next day will be dry and sunny.

Some plants can be used to **forecast** the weather. These African marigolds close their colorful petals when it is going to rain.

Weather Patterns

We use photographs of Earth taken from space to find patterns in the weather. Clouds show that a storm is coming. No clouds show that it is dry.

People use these patterns to figure out what the weather will be. We can see weather **forecasts** on television or in the newspapers.

How Much Rain?

Special airplanes fly into clouds to measure the amount of water inside the clouds. This helps people know how much rain will fall.

This man is using a **rain gauge**. It collects rain and shows how much rain has fallen.

Which Way Is the Wind Blowing?

Watching the way the wind blows helps people understand how the weather may change. This **weather vane** shows the wind is blowing from the south.

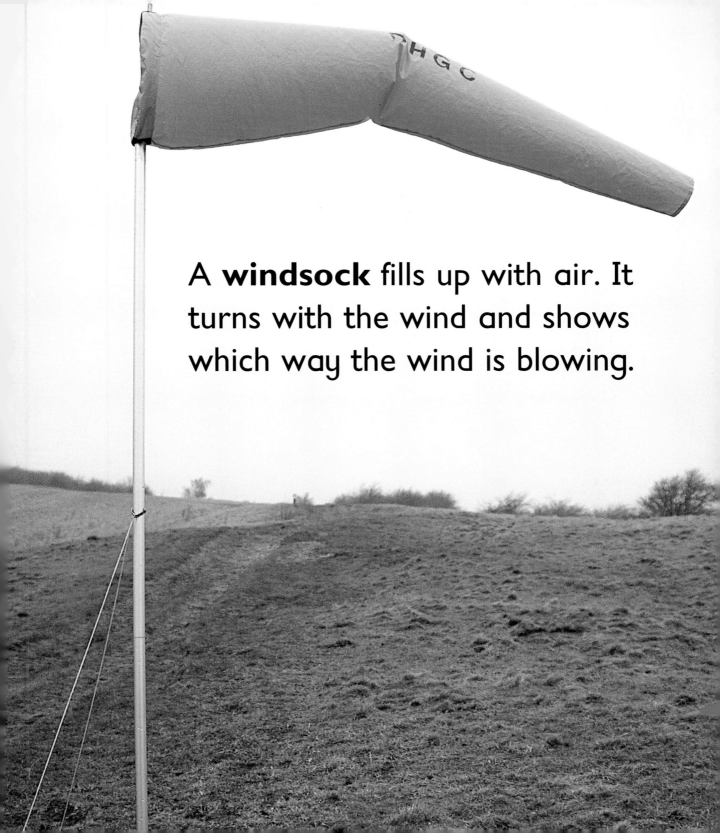

A **windsock** fills up with air. It turns with the wind and shows which way the wind is blowing.

How Fast Is the Wind?

Wind fills these large sails and pushes the boats. The harder it blows, the faster the boats move.

These cups catch wind and spin
around. They measure how fast
the wind is blowing. Here, the wind
is blowing at more than six feet
(two meters) a second.

Weather Balloons

This balloon carries machines that watch the weather. It will fly higher than any airplane. We can learn what the weather is like high above the ground.

The balloon sends messages about wind and rain. People use computers to look at these messages. Then they know how the weather will change.

Watching from Space

Satellites in space watch the weather on Earth. They send messages and photos back to Earth. This information teaches us more about the weather.

The earth looks blue from space. But the colors of this **satellite photo** have been changed by a computer. The bright colors show where it is raining.

Weather Warning

Warnings are given if the weather is going to be very bad. Forecasters try to **forecast** the weather so people are ready when bad weather comes.

These people have heard a danger warning. They are using bags of sand to stop water from flooding into their houses after heavy rain.

Danger!

This is a **satellite photo** of a storm. Messages on television and radio warn people who are in danger from the storm.

These people were in the building to get away from a dangerous storm. They were safe inside until the wind and rain had passed.

Weather Long Ago

The weather slowly changes. These old paintings in the Sahara **Desert** show that giraffes once lived there. But now this place is too dry and dusty for giraffes.

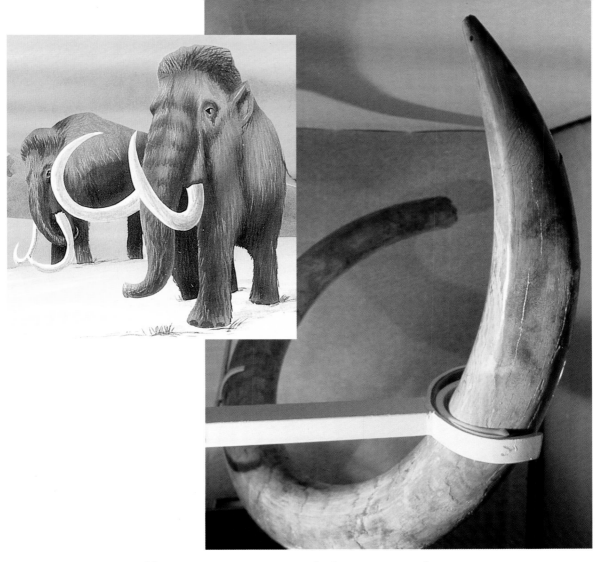

This woolly mammoth's tooth was found in England. Woolly mammoths lived long ago in cold, icy places. So we know that England was once much colder than it is now.

Changing Weather

The weather is still changing. **Antarctica** is covered in thick ice. But much of the ice is melting. Is the world getting warmer?

Things that happen on Earth can change the weather. Clouds of ash from this huge **volcano** blocked the heat from the sun. This made it cooler everywhere for a few years.

It's Amazing!

Strong winds called the *jet stream* blow high above the ground. They blow at over 120 miles (200 kilometers) per hour. Airplanes use the power of the jet stream to fly faster.

In Peru, the weather **forecast** is the most popular program on television.

Supermarkets need to know what the weather will be. People buy more ice cream and cold drinks when the weather is hot.

Glossary

Antarctica   land at the southernmost part of the world, around the South Pole

desert   place where there is very little rain

forecast   information that tells what the weather may be

rain gauge   tube that collects rain to show how much has fallen

satellite   spacecraft that moves around the earth

satellite photo   photograph taken in space from a satellite

volcano   hole in the earth's surface through which melted rock, ash, and gases escape

waterproof   able to keep water out

weather vane   device that turns in the wind to show which way the wind is blowing

windsock   type of bag or sleeve that shows which way the wind is blowing

More Books to Read

Casey, Denise. *Weather Everywhere*. New York: Simon & Schuster Children's, 1995.

Hopkins, Lee B. (ed.) *Weather*. New York: HarperCollins Children's Books, 1994.

Rowe, Julian and Molly Perham. *Weather Watch!* Danbury, Conn: Children's Press, 1998.

Index